REVEALED

UNMASKING FAMILIAR SPIRITS

KAKRA BAIDEN

DEDICATION

To Samuel Sawyerr. I appreciate your friendship.

TABLE OF CONTENTS

INTRODUCTION

My people are destroyed for lack of knowledge.
—Hosea 4:6

Have you ever come across someone who alienated himself from his family because of a so-called spiritual experience? Can you explain why a "godly dream" would make someone amputate the hands of his own sister? Have you ever had a dream where someone wanted to have an affair with you? If you answered yes to any of these questions you could be dealing with a familiar spirit.

They are a category of evil spirits whose activities have remained largely undetected because of the lack of information concerning them. As a result some Christians have become victims of these shadowy spirits with disastrous consequences. Through deception they can destroy marriages, families, and even churches.

This book will reveal the nature and activities of familiar spirits by using the Scriptures, visions, and personal experience. It will help you understand, identify, and defeat them in the name of Jesus.

1

THE TRANCE

I was pacing up and down my room in prayer around 4 a.m. when I fell into a trance. I was suddenly transported into the spirit realm. The word "trance" comes form the Greek word *ekstasis*, which means to have your natural senses suspended.

The walls of my room became transparent like glass and amazingly I could see the compound of my house. On my lawn I saw two angels with three white horses. The third horse did not seem to have a rider.

They beckoned me to come. Surprisingly I didn't go through the door; it seemed I just walked through the wall. I realized it's a real thing when the Bible says, "We shall be partakers of the powers of the world to come" (see Hebrews 6:4-5). Such experiences are recorded in the Scriptures.

For instance, did you know Jesus could vanish? One day He stepped into a boat and the whole boat appeared on the shore, "Then they willingly received him into the ship: and immediately the ship was at the land whither they went" (John 6:21).

Can you imagine if you could just vanish without having to purchase a plane ticket or spend long hours at an airport? That would be great. That's why we must not miss heaven. Now back to my vision.

I sat on the riderless horse and immediately we took off. The horses seemed to travel at great speed and the scenery changed rapidly. We travelled through forests, cities, deserts, etc. These horses could even gallop on the sea.

At one point there seemed to be a hideous creature pursuing us. The angels explained to me that it was an evil spirit. We managed to lose this creature by going behind a big tree and we saw it blindly rush past. Finally we stopped in a thick forest. I asked the angels why they had brought me there and they explained they wanted to show me how familiar spirits operated.

Suddenly the ground opened and we went down a deep shaft. Down and down we descended into the earth. We arrived in a circular room with little pieces of wood stacked in a great pile.

One of the angel said to me, "Pick some." I picked three pieces of wood and saw names on them. I could not recognize the first two names but I recognized the last name. It was the name of a pastor I had heard about but did not know personally.

The angel said to me, "Every piece of wood has a name written on it, and they are the names of ministers of God who use familiar spirits. They come from underground and we wanted to show you their source." I was speechless. I tried to take more of the pieces of wood, but they told me I could not pick anymore. I will explain the significance of this vision later.

2

MY PEOPLE ARE DESTROYED

My people are destroyed for lack of knowledge.
—Hosea 4:6

Recently the Lord spoke to me and said, "The church of God has been overrun by familiar spirits; it has become like a dog with ticks."

I said, "Lord, why has the church been infested with familiar spirits?"

He responded, "Ignorance! Wherever ignorance thrives, the devil will reign."

We can be children of God and still be destroyed because of spiritual illiteracy. The cure to this is knowledge. The knowledge and application of the Word of God releases the power of God.

The Example of Jesus

> And it came to pass on a certain day, as he was teaching, that there were Pharisees and doctors of the law sitting by, which were come out of every town of Galilee, and Judaea, and Jerusalem: and the power of the Lord was present to heal them.　　—Luke 5:17

As Jesus was teaching we are told "the power of the Lord was present to heal them." The teaching of God's Word is a trigger that releases the power of God. That is why you are going to be transformed by this book. Let me give you an example of what teaching can do.

Growth Healed

One day a man who had a growth on his head for twenty years came to one of my meetings. After I finished preaching, he was on his way home when he felt something wet and sticky on his neck. When he touched it he saw blood. The growth had suddenly burst.

When he woke up the following morning the growth had vanished, the sore had healed, and a scar formed overnight. The teaching of God's Word had released the healing power of God. By the time you finish reading this book I believe the power of any familiar spirit that may be operating in your life will be broken.

3

SAUL'S ENCOUNTER WITH A FAMILIAR SPIRIT

And when Saul saw the host of the Philistines, he was afraid, and his heart greatly trembled. And when Saul enquired of the LORD, the LORD answered him not, neither by dreams, nor by Urim, nor by prophets.

Then said Saul unto his servants, Seek me a woman that hath a familiar spirit, that I may go to her, and enquire of her. And his servants said to him, Behold, there is a woman that hath a familiar spirit at Endor. And Saul disguised himself, and put on other raiment, and he went, and two men with him, and they came to the woman by night: and he said, I pray thee,

divine unto me by the familiar spirit, and bring
me him up, whom I shall name unto thee.

—1 Samuel 28:5-8

I got to know about familiar spirits after I gave my
life to Christ. Familiar spirits used to be a mysterious subject to me. A mystery is something that is
difficult to understand.

I used to ask fellow Christians what a familiar spirit
was. I received answers like, "Oh! They are spirits who
are familiar with you. They know you." I found the
answers unsatisfactory. I would say to myself, *Are we
studying English grammar or what?* Over the years God
has granted me knowledge through His Word and
visions about this mysterious class of demons.

When God spoke to me about this I said to myself,
Let me check if there is a book on familiar spirits. I
googled and I couldn't find one book, not even one
on this subject. The Lord said to me, "That is why I
want you to write about them."

WE ALL FACE PROBLEMS

It does not matter whether you are poor or rich,
young or old, one day you will come across a problem
that is bigger than you are. A problem that money,
connections, nor medical science can solve. This
is how Job summarized life: "Man that is born of a
woman is of few days, and full of trouble" (Job 14:1).

Saul was a king, but one day he faced a Philistine army that was stronger and bigger than the army of Israel, "When Saul saw the host of the Philistines, he was afraid, and his heart greatly trembled" (1 Samuel 28:5). He realized he was no match for this superior army. Fear gripped his heart and he started trembling. Fear is an emotion, and trembling is the physical expression of that internal emotion.

GOD CAN SPEAK THROUGH DREAMS

One of the ways God speaks to us is through dreams, "For God speaketh once, yea twice.... In a dream, in a vision of the night" (Job 33:14-15). Saul's first reaction was to pray for guidance through dreams but he did not receive any response, "And when Saul enquired of the LORD, the LORD answered him not, neither by dreams" (1 Samuel 28:6).

Sometimes when we need guidance from the Lord we pray and hope that God will speak to us through dreams. It could be a major decision like who to marry or whether to take a particular job offer. You can be frustrated when it seems you can't get an answer to your deep needs.

GOD CAN SPEAK THROUGH URIM AND THUMMIM

God did not speak to Saul by Urim or Thummim, "The Lord answered him not, neither by Urim nor by Thummim" (1 Samuel 28:6). Urim means perfection and Thummim means light. These were two stones that were fixed on the robes of the high priest. They were placed around the area of the breast and were used to interpret the will of God.

I believe these stones symbolize the conviction of the Holy Spirit to the modern-day Christian. We must be led by the conviction of the Holy Spirit. This conviction must be based on the light of the Scriptures (Thummim) and perfection or holiness (Urim). This means any conviction we have that is not based on the Word or holiness of God is not from God.

This is because you can develop wrong convictions and happens when you ignore the conviction of God in small matters. Over time your conviction is corrupted and you are no longer sensitive to the voice of the Spirit. Saul had no guidance through the Holy Spirit either.

God Can Speak through Prophecy

"The Lord answered him not by ... prophets." I believe this refers to the Word of God, "We have also a more sure word of prophecy" (2 Peter 1:19). It could also mean a personal word from the Lord. Saul did not receive any direction from either a word from the Lord or personal prophecies.

Have you ever prayed and felt God was far from you? Maybe you were believing God for a baby, a spouse, a job, or the salvation of your family, but you received no answer. You have fasted and prayed but heaven remains silent. Meanwhile the clock is ticking, tick tock, and time is running out on your opportunities, and sometimes life itself.

4

DESPERATE PEOPLE TAKE DESPERATE MEASURES

Then said Saul unto his servants, Seek me a woman that hath a familiar spirit, that I may go to her, and enquire of her. And his servants said to him, Behold, there is a woman that hath a familiar spirit at Endor.

And Saul disguised himself, and put on other raiment, and he went, and two men with him, and they came to the woman by night: and he said, I pray thee, divine unto me by the familiar spirit, and bring me him up, whom I shall name unto thee.   —1 Samuel 28:7-8

The devil likes desperate people because desperate people can take desperate measures. Have you noticed that when you are hungry, even food you may not particularly like suddenly looks nice and inviting? "The full soul loatheth an honeycomb; but to the hungry soul every bitter thing is sweet" (Proverbs 27:7). Desperation can make you do things you never imagined you could do.

DESPERATION AND BAD COUNSEL

One of Saul's servants, under great pressure, took advantage of Saul's desperation and advised him to seek counsel from a familiar spirit. Previously Saul had killed all witches who dabbled in familiar spirits. Is it not interesting that sometimes we can set standards for people to follow but when we find ourselves in the same circumstances we capitulate? Saul could not follow his own prescribed rules. It is also interesting to note that sometimes you may think you share the same values with someone but in a time of crisis you discover you don't share the same values at all.

Unknown to Saul there was an undercover consulter of familiar spirits in his inner circle. Someone in his own house was still dealing with familiar spirits.

Anyone can claim to have your back in good times, but crisis has a way of revealing who your true friends are. Don't call people friends until they have been tested; maybe they are acquaintances. Fire will always separate the true followers of Christ from the crowd.

The devil likes to offer counsel when we are under pressure, and he likes using people, especially trusted ones, as his mouthpiece. He can even use family members or fellow church members.

When you have a serious marital problem with your spouse, the devil can take advantage of the situation and use someone to counsel you. The person may say, "Pack your things and leave! If it were me, I would have left a long time ago. I can't stand such nonsense."

THE EXAMPLE OF JESUS

Satan counseled Jesus to turn stones into bread after He had fasted for forty days because he knew He was hungry and desperately needed food, "Being forty days tempted of the devil. And in those days he did eat nothing: and when they were ended, he afterward hungered. And the devil said unto him, If thou be the Son of God, command this stone that it be made bread" (Luke 4:2-3).

Be careful not to satisfy your immediate needs at the expense of your long-term future. Our needs and emotions must be subjected to the Word of God, and Saul failed to do that.

DESPERATION AND VULNERABILITY

Our weakest moments are often the times of our greatest vulnerability. Delilah took advantage of Samson's emotional vulnerability towards her to sell the secret of his strength to five kings for 5,500 pieces of silver. Compare that to Judas who sold Jesus for thirty pieces of silver. Delilah surely was a more cunning businesswoman. Delilah struck when Samson was most vulnerable. His eyes were closed and he was fast asleep on her lap. Be careful which lap you rest your head on.

In Saul's desperation he opened himself up to receive counsel from an unusual source. One of his servants seized upon his vulnerability to counsel him. He was prepared to sacrifice his relationship with God to maintain his power. As you read on you will also discover the witch took advantage of Saul's desperation to prophesy his death.

In times of trouble there will always be people who would like to take advantage of you emotionally, financially, and even sexually. Do not be desperate for power, money, promotion, or even love, because when you are desperate, people can easily take advantage of you.

DESPERATE FOR LOVE

I knew a woman who was desperate to get married. All her boyfriends exploited her financially and eventually dumped her. When you are desperate for promotion in an office environment it can make you vulnerable to manipulation by your superiors. You can abandon your values and beliefs and become an actor in your own life. With such good acting you may even win an Oscar.

It is important to have faith in God because you are protected from exploitation, "The name of the LORD is a strong tower: the righteous runneth into it, and is safe" (Proverbs 18:10). Trust in the Lord.

DESPERATION AND DECEPTION

Saul was easily deceived by the witch. He was made to believe he was communicating with Samuel when he was in actual fact communicating with a familiar spirit.

I have seen many spiritually gullible people deceived by psychics, so-called prophets, and men of God because they sensed their desperation. There are some people who want to hear something by all means. If you want to hear something by all means you will hear by all means something, but it may not necessarily be the voice of God.

DESPERATION AND THE OCCULT

I met a Christian brother who was so desperate to be wealthy he had gone to consult the occult. He was told to sacrifice one of his fingers for the rites. I advised him against it and asked him to be patient with the Lord. Fortunately he listened to me. The devil likes desperate people because desperate people take desperate measures. Saul consulted the occult because he needed answers by hook or by crook.

5

PRAYER VERSUS WAITING

Be not slothful, but followers of them who through faith and patience inherit the promises.
—Hebrews 6:12

Do you know that it's more difficult to wait than to pray? One way to overcome desperation is to be patient. What God wanted from Saul was not prayer but patience. Sometimes the answers to our problems do not necessarily lie in our prayers but in our waiting.

Many blessings have come when I have just waited for the promises of God to manifest. Sometimes a pastor can pray for church growth but instead the church size decreases. You can pray for money and lose your job. You could be praying to God for a baby and suffer a miscarriage.

A woman told me, "Pastor, I am thirty-one and have no husband, and when I went to the hospital, I was told I have fibroids. So what should I do? I am being pressured to have a baby out of wedlock." I can understand the pressure, but patience is still needed.

Someone may say, "The Lord's name is the Ancient of Days and He does not grow, but I do. Therefore, if He doesn't give me someone to marry now, I will marry Spiderman." Hey! The key is still patience. Your time will come. Trust in the Lord with all your heart and lean not on your own understanding. It takes faith and patience to inherit the promises.

When it's winter you don't pray for summer to come. You just wait for the season to change. Sometimes all you can do is sit still and wait for your season to change because no amount of prayer can change it, "Be patient therefore, brethren, unto the coming of the Lord. Behold, the husbandman waiteth for the precious fruit of the earth, and hath long patience for it, until he receive the early and latter rain" (James 5:7).

Abraham waited twenty-five years to have a baby, "After he had patiently endured he obtained the promise" (Hebrews 6:15). Not after he had patiently fasted or prayed all night, but after he had patiently *endured*, he obtained the promise. Do you know it is more difficult to wait than to pray? Saul couldn't wait; avoid the same mistake.

6

Deception and Impersonation

Then the King said to the woman, What sawest thou? And the woman said unto Saul, I saw gods ascending out of the earth. And he said unto her, What form is he of? And she said, An old man cometh up; and he is covered with a mantle. And Saul perceived that it was Samuel, and he stooped with his face to the ground, and bowed himself.   —1 Samuel 28:13-14

The main job of familiar spirits is to deceive us and ultimately lead us away from the Lord. Jesus warned that deception will be one of the main tools of the devil in the last days, and I believe that familiar spirits are at the vanguard of this, "And Jesus answered and said unto them, Take heed that no man deceive you" (Matthew 24:4). What distinguishes them is their modus operandi: they deceive people through impersonation.

IMPERSONATION

To impersonate means to take on the identity of someone else. Whilst preaching in New York a woman said to me, "Pastor, how did your wife's operation in Germany go?"

I asked, "My wife? What operation in Germany?"

"Oh! Don't you remember? You said your wife was going to Germany to have surgery and you didn't have enough money to cover the cost so we should help you raise money. My friends and I sent some money to help you."

I replied, "My wife did not go to Germany. She is at home."

She said, "Oh Pastor, were you not the one I spoke with on the phone and told me I should raise money to help you?"

I replied, "It was not me."

She exclaimed, "Ahh! Someone has deceived me!"

Somebody had impersonated me. The person took on my identity and raised money in my name. I started thinking, *If people can even use my name to deceive others, what about the name of Jesus?*

Why was this woman deceived? The answer is simple: impersonation. If the impersonator had asked the women for money for himself, he would have been rejected. But because he used my identity he managed to deceive and dupe them.

In Saul's case they deceived him into thinking he was communicating with Samuel when he was actually communicating with familiar spirits. Eventually Saul backslid, and he and his two sons were killed by the Philistines.

7

FAMILIAR SPIRITS IMPERSONATE DEAD PEOPLE

One morning I woke up to discover many missed calls from a pastor friend of mine. He had been calling me since dawn. I wondered, *Ah! Why is this pastor calling me like that?* When I called back he said he desperately wanted to see me, so I asked him to come over. When he came I asked, "Pastor, what's wrong?"

He said, "Pastor, they are calling me."

I said, "Who and where?"

He answered, "I had a vivid dream early this morning. In the dream, a friend of mine who recently died came to my bedroom and said, 'I have been sent to come and call you.' I asked, 'Where?' He answered, 'the cemetery.' I asked, 'When?' and he answered, 'Now.'" At that point he woke up with great fear and that was when he started calling me. He was so scared he was going to die.

I believe the person he saw was not his friend but a familiar spirit who had impersonated his friend. He knew that if he came as a demon, he would be recognized. So he came as his friend, and of course, he spoke with him.

That's what happened to Saul. A familiar spirit appeared as Samuel, Saul's spiritual father who had died some time ago. Saul believed everything that "Samuel" said because he thought it was Samuel. But it wasn't Samuel; it was a familiar spirit. Why was it not Samuel but a familiar spirit?

> And the king said unto her, Be not afraid: for what sawest thou? And the woman said unto Saul, I saw gods ascending out of the earth. And he said unto her, What form is he of? And she said, An old man cometh up; and he is covered with a mantle. And Saul perceived that it was Samuel, and he stooped with his face to the ground, and bowed himself.
>
> —1 Samuel 28:13-14

THE SOURCE OF THE SPIRITS

Saul asked the woman, "What sawest thou?" And the woman said unto Saul, "I saw gods ascending out of the earth." These spirits first appeared as gods, which were lesser or evil spirits. But by the time they manifested they had all metamorphosed into the image of a single individual, Samuel, "An old man cometh up; and he is covered with a mantle. And Saul perceived that it was Samuel" (1 Samuel 28:14). The source of the spirits was demonic.

THE VERDICT OF GOD

God Himself said He was not involved with anything that Saul saw and heard. The whole experience wasn't from Him. God Himself explained why Saul died, "So Saul died for his transgression which he committed against the LORD, even against the word of the LORD, which he kept not, and also for asking counsel of one that had a familiar spirit, to enquire of it; and enquired not of the LORD: therefore he slew him, and turned the kingdom unto David the son of Jesse" (1 Chronicles 10:13-14).

Saul died because he did not enquire or seek answers from God. God had nothing to do with all that Saul saw and heard. So why was Saul deceived? Very simple! Because the familiar spirit impersonated a dead person that Saul loved and respected. For his punishment God slew him: "therefore He slew him and turned the kingdom again to David, the son of Jesse."

Is It Normal to Dream About Dead People?

> There shall not be found among you any one
> that maketh his son or his daughter to pass
> through the fire, or that useth divination, or an
> observer of times, or an enchanter, or a witch,
> or a charmer, or a consulter with familiar spirits,
> or a wizard, or a necromancer.
>
> —Deuteronomy 18:10-11

Necromancy, which is talking to the spirits of dead people, is forbidden in the Scriptures. Notice the other things that are in the same company: soothsaying or divination, astrology or an observer of times, witchcraft, etc. If necromancy is allowed, all these should also be allowed because they are in the same company.

From the Scripture it seems to me it's not normal to be communicating with the dead in dreams. It seems to be an exception rather than a rule. It's like walking on water; it's an exception rather than a rule.

Why am I saying that? I personally recall one instance in the New Testament where the dead communicated with the living. At the transfiguration of Jesus two dead people appeared to Him: Moses and Elijah, "And, behold, there appeared unto them Moses and Elias talking with him" (Matthew 17:1-3). But the general principle is the dead do not normally communicate with the living, but this is an exceptional case.

Owusu the Carpenter

I knew a carpenter called Owusu who used to make repairs in my house. One day he died. After he died I saw him in a dream. He came to my house and asked me if I wanted him to repair anything. I said, "Owusu, how much are you going to charge me?"

He replied, "I won't charge you. It is free."

I asked him, "Who are you?"

Immediately I knew I was not talking to Owusu because the Owusu I knew never worked for free or gave discounts. The minute I said that he froze and ran out of the house. I felt a familiar spirit had just made an attempt to enter my house by impersonating Owusu.

LESSONS ON DEATH AS TOLD BY JESUS

And beside all this, between us and you there is a great gulf fixed: so that they which would pass from hence to you cannot; neither can they pass to us, that would come from thence. Then he said, I pray thee therefore, father, that thou wouldest send him to my father's house: for I have five brethren; that he may testify unto them, lest they also come into this place of torment. Abraham saith unto him, They have Moses and the prophets; let them hear them.

—Luke 16:26-29

In the story of Lazarus and the rich man, the rich man told Abraham to send Lazarus with a message to his five brothers to tell them about hell. Abraham replied that it was impossible for the dead to communicate with the living because of a great gulf that existed between the two. So if the dead cannot cross to the living, who are these dead people who have been communicating in dreams and visions?

My Friend Whose Sister Died of Cancer

I have a friend whose sister died of cancer. After her death he dreamt about her. In the dream, his sister came to his bedroom to lie by his side and chat. After a while his sister lay on top of him, opened his mouth, and put her mouth on his mouth. She started vomiting into his mouth till his stomach became full. Afterwards the dead sister rose up, walked to the door, turned and changed into the form of an evil spirit, and then disappeared. The familiar spirit was able to gain access to him by impersonation.

Lessons on Death As Told by Paul

But I would not have you to be ignorant, brethren, concerning them which are asleep, that ye sorrow not, even as others which have no hope. For if we believe that Jesus died and rose again, even so them also which sleep in Jesus will God bring with him.

—1 Thessalonians 4:13-14

For the Lord himself shall descend from heaven with a shout, with the voice of the archangel, and with the trump of God: and the dead in Christ shall rise first.   —1 Thessalonians 4:16

Paul said Jesus would descend from heaven to call the dead from their grave. So if God is not calling the dead, who is calling these dead people? It is not time for the resurrection of the dead, so why are the dead walking around? I believe many are familiar spirits, ministering to people in dreams. Anyone who claims he is calling your dead relative to communicate with you is using a familiar spirit.

8

FAMILIAR SPIRITS IMPERSONATE HEAVENLY BEINGS

But I fear, lest by any means, as the serpent beguiled Eve through his subtilty, so your minds should be corrupted from the simplicity that is in Christ.   —2 Corinthians 11:3

For such are false apostles, deceitful workers, transforming themselves into the apostles of Christ. And no marvel; for Satan himself is transformed into an angel of light. Therefore it is no great thing if his ministers also be transformed as the ministers of righteousness; whose end shall be according to their works.

—2 Corinthians 11:13-15

One reason why the devil was able to deceive Eve was because he took on another form: the form of a serpent. Originally he was a fallen angel. Eve engaged him in conversation because she thought she was conversing with one of the creatures in the garden, "The serpent beguiled Eve through his subtilty."

Paul was concerned about the church of Corinth because he felt they were susceptible to deception through impersonation, "For such are false apostles, deceitful workers, transforming themselves into the apostles of Christ. And no marvel; for Satan can transform himself into an angel of light."

There are two types of angels: angels with light and angels without light. Angels without light are fallen angels. They have no light because they are not holy. Holiness emits a light, and that is why God is light.

In the book of Job, Satan managed to appear before God undetected because he impersonated an angel of light, "Now there was a day when the sons of God came to present themselves before the Lord, and Satan came also among them" (Job 1:6). God was able to identify him, but his fellow angels could not. If even angels can be deceived, you can imagine how vigilant we must be.

I Am Supposed to Marry My Pastor

A woman told me an angel had appeared to her saying she was supposed to marry her pastor. The pastor was already married, so she was praying for the pastor to leave his wife and marry her. I asked, "How is this possible?"

She said, "The angel told me my pastor's marriage was registered on earth but not in heaven." She continued, "In heaven it's my name that is registered, but my pastor's wife's name is on the earthly register. So I am on a twenty-one-day fast to reclaim my husband."

I said to her, "That thing is not an angel; it is a familiar spirit masquerading as an angel. Jesus said there are no marriages in heaven." "But they which shall be accounted worthy to obtain that world, and the resurrection from the dead, neither marry, nor are given in marriage" (Luke 20:35).

Relationships, homes, marriages, and even churches have broken apart because of such satanic manifestations. Confusion, strife, and separation have characterized such experiences.

MY EXPERIENCE WITH SATAN

Whilst praying one morning around 3 a.m. I saw the heavens open. I saw angels descending from heaven and singing, "Hail the Lord! Hail the Lord!" They formed two lines and created a corridor, and I saw Jesus in the middle walking towards me. I said, "Oh! I'm blessed! Today Jesus has come to bless me!" I went down on my knees and started worshipping.

When He got close to me, I saw the border of His white robe but it was not shining. It looked like ordinary cloth. I've seen Jesus several times and He radiates light. I remember once asking Him why He shone and He said it was the color of holiness. I started thinking in my head, *What kind of Jesus is this? Maybe it's a Chinese Jesus.*

CHINESE JESUS

There is a certain film in which Jesus is a Chinese man. As He was being crucified on the cross, the bystanders started laughing and mocking the Chinese Jesus. He warned them to stop; otherwise He would come down from the cross and beat them up. They did not heed His warnings and continued laughing, as you may be laughing by now. He gave a second warning but they continued mocking. Then He shook His head and cried, "Keaaaaa!" He jumped down from the cross and beat them up.

I was wondering, *What Chinese Jesus is this who has no glory?* I lifted my eyes to look and my eyes met two big green eyes. My blood curdled within me, and my heart skipped a beat. The hair on my skin rose because I knew I was looking at Satan, eyeball to eyeball.

I shouted, *Jesus!* There was a large explosion, bang! Like somebody had thrown a bomb, and immediately the devil and all his angels were blown away by the name of Jesus. I was almost deceived by the devil while his hand was inches away from my head.

THE WOMAN IN MY CHURCH

A woman in our church told me about a dream she had. In the dream, an angel came to her and told her I was not a good pastor because I was in the occult. That was why God was working miracles by my hand. I explained to her it was a familiar spirit. A lot of discernment is needed in the spirit realm. That's why some people break up churches and some start cults.

When Jesus fasted for forty days, the first person to appear was the devil—not the Holy Spirit. You would think the devil would run away from someone who was fasting. He was there the whole forty days. But you see, he knew the Word of God, so his judgment and response were based on it.

Families have been destroyed, good friends are no longer friends, children don't talk to parents, people in the same church are fighting, and churches have broken up because a familiar spirit impersonated somebody in a dream.

9

FAMILIAR SPIRITS IMPERSONATE LIVING PEOPLE

And no marvel; for Satan himself is transformed into an angel of light. Therefore it is no great thing if his ministers also be transformed as the ministers of righteousness; whose end shall be according to their works.

—2 Corinthians 11:14-15

The ministers of Satan are both human and spirit, and we are told they can transform themselves. Familiar spirits can impersonate the living, not only the dead. Whether they are alive or not does not make a difference. The principle is they can manifest in human form.

Identifying People in Dreams

Who are you really dealing with when you see someone you know in your dreams? The ability to know who you are dealing with in a dream is crucial because it will determine your understanding and response. There are several possibilities.

1. Actual Person

I received a letter from a woman who had been hospitalized with a serious heart condition. She said Jesus appeared to her, mentioned my name, and showed her my picture. He told her the city where I lived and the church I pastored. He asked her to send for me because if I prayed she would be healed. I went to see her.

I was wondering how I could identify her because I did not know her. When I entered the hospital ward she called me by name and rose to meet me. I asked her how she was able to recognize me. She told me Jesus showed her my picture. I prayed for her and she was miraculously healed and discharged within three days.

Saul had a similar experience when he met Jesus on the road to Damascus. He became blind after the experience. A certain disciple named Ananias was asked to pray for Saul and restore his sight. Saul saw Ananias in a vision before he came to pray for him, "And hath seen in a vision a man named Ananias coming in, and putting his hand on him, that he might receive his sight" (Acts 9:12). The person Saul saw was the actual person. That is why you can see an actual person in a dream or vision.

2. SPIRIT OF THE PERSON

I had a dream about someone I knew. In this dream he was trying to stab me with a knife. It did not literally mean the person was going to stab me because I did not think he was capable of that. It just revealed the hatred he had for me, "Whosoever hateth his brother is a murderer: and ye know that no murderer hath eternal life abiding in him" (1 John 3:15). This Scripture equates hatred, which is an emotional or spiritual condition, with murder.

The spirit of a man looks exactly like him. In the story of Lazarus and the rich man, they recognized themselves in death. Meanwhile they had both been buried, "And it came to pass, that the beggar died, and was carried by the angels into Abraham's bosom: the rich man also died, and was buried; And in hell he lift up his eyes, being in torments, and seeth Abraham afar off, and Lazarus in his bosom" (Luke 16:22-23).

Because of this you may have a dream and see the spirit of someone. Such dreams may reveal the inner nature of a person; his mind, character, spirit, intentions, etc. It does not necessarily mean the spirit will physically manifest.

3. Familiar Spirit

I know of a church where someone amputated the hands of his own sister because of a dream he had. Life had not been going well for this young man. He had a dream and saw his sister as the source of all his problems. He concluded his sister was a witch.

When he woke up he took a machete and amputated the hands of his own sister. Do you think the Holy Spirit would advise someone to amputate his own sister's hands? The person he saw in the dream was not his sister; it was a familiar spirit.

A woman once said to me, "My two sisters and I don't talk to my mother. As for me, since I gave birth, my mother has not even seen my children."

I asked, "Why?"

She said, "I saw my mother in a dream try to kill me and my sisters."

I said, "I just want to ask you a question. Since you were born, has your mother been a good or bad mother? Has she done evil to you?"

She said, "No, my mother has been a very good mother. But since we had this dream, Pastor, we are afraid of her."

I continued, "If your mother wanted to kill someone, you would not be alive. She would have killed you when you were young. It would have been easier." Then I said, "You need two or three witnesses to confirm a word. God didn't say it was only by their dreams that you would know them. He also said by their fruits you would know them. The fruit that your mother has exhibited is far greater than the dream." I advised her to seek forgiveness from her mother because she had allowed a familiar spirit to destroy their relationship. Familiar spirits have destroyed many homes, relationships, marriages, and friendships.

FAMILIAR SPIRITS AND SEXUAL ENCOUNTERS

I knew a woman who had experienced multiple miscarriages. Any time she conceived she would dream and see herself having sex with a particular person. After the encounter she would miscarry the baby. When I prayed for her, the sexual encounters ceased and she conceived and gave birth successfully. I am convinced she was sleeping with a familiar spirit in the guise of a human being.

Sometimes people dream and find themselves in sexual acts with people they know. I am convinced some of these people are familiar spirits disguised in human form, "Likewise also these filthy dreamers defile the flesh, despise dominion, and speak evil of dignities" (Jude 1:8).

Paul calls such people filthy dreamers. Filthy dreams can cause you to defile your flesh with spirits. Our flesh can be defiled not only in physical sexual encounters but also in dreams.

I have a theory, which I believe explains why familiar spirits like taking on human form. You are free to agree or disagree with it. I may even be wrong. I believe they love manifesting as humans because humans were made from the ground. They also come from underground so they try to mimic us, "And the LORD God formed man out of the dust of the ground. He breathed into his nostrils the breath of life; and man became a living soul" (Genesis 2:7).

10

DIVINATION

Then said Saul unto his servants, Seek me a woman that hath a familiar spirit, that I may go to her, and enquire of her. And his servants said to him, Behold, there is a woman that hath a familiar spirit at Endor. And Saul disguised himself, and put on other raiment, and he went, and two men with him, and they came to the woman by night: and he said, I pray thee, divine unto me by the familiar spirit, and bring me him up, whom I shall name unto thee.

—1 Samuel 28:7-8

Saul's request was specific. He said, "Divine unto me by the familiar spirit." Familiar spirits possess powers of divination. What does divination mean?

First it means to have supernatural knowledge, and secondly it means to be able to predict the future. Let's examine these definitions more closely.

Divination means to have supernatural knowledge. The witch had supernatural knowledge about events in Saul's life even though she was not present when they occurred. In a previous battle God had instructed Saul to kill all the Amalekites and destroy everything. But Saul spared the king, Agag, and some of the valuables. The witch reminded Saul of this event and his disobedience towards God, "Because thou obeyedst not the voice of the LORD, nor executedst his fierce wrath upon Amalek, therefore hath the LORD done this thing unto thee this day" (1 Samuel 28:18). How could someone who was not present or part of the army know such things? She had the power of divination.

SPIRITUAL GIFTS AND DECEPTION

This is where many Christians are deceived. The fact that somebody possesses supernatural knowledge does not make him a man of God. There is a genuine spiritual gift, a word of knowledge, which God gave to the church, "For to one is given by the Spirit the word of wisdom; to another the word of knowledge by the same Spirit" (1 Corinthians 12:8).

There are many times when I have known things supernaturally. There are times God has revealed details of people's lives or experiences to me in dreams, visions, and revelations.

Once a pastor told me he did not understand why his ministry was not doing well so he wanted me to pray with him. The following day I had a long vision concerning him. One of the reasons was adultery. In this vision he went to preach for another pastor friend and ended up sleeping with his wife. When I told him of this he was shocked and admitted it was true. I asked him to repent.

THE COUNTERFEIT OF THIS IS DIVINATION

The operation of divination is the same but the source is different. The source of divination is not God but other spirits. Psychics use divination.

A familiar spirit can mention your name, address, and telephone number. Charismatic Christians can be so gullible that when somebody has supernatural knowledge they immediately conclude the person is of God. The Bible does not say by their *gifts* you shall know them; it says by their *fruit* you shall know them. What makes someone a Christian is not his gifts but his fruit or character, "Ye shall know them by their fruits. Do men gather grapes of thorns, or figs of this-tles?" (Matthew 7:16). The devil has power, but he does not have the fruit of the Spirit because his nature is essentially evil. That is why he cannot manifest the fruit of the Spirit.

Familiar spirits use supernatural knowledge to deceive, convince, and influence. If you possess supernatural knowledge, you can easily convince spiritually gullible people that you are of God and win their confidence. They will say, "If it's not God, how could he or she have known this?"

Once you give people one accurate word of knowledge, they immediately assume that you are of God and everything else you say is coming from God. From that time they want to use you as a spiritual ATM machine to dispense prophecy.

I once had a vision about someone. I told him his whole life history: the circumstances of his birth and what he had been through. The person was so impressed he started bugging me for more revelations. If I had told him God said he should give me a thousand dollars he would have believed it because I had won his confidence. I have seen people manipulated by some "ministers of God" through this means.

Paul and the Young Girl in Ephesus

And it came to pass, as we went to prayer, a certain damsel possessed with a spirit of divination met us, which brought her masters much gain by soothsaying: the same followed Paul and us, and cried, saying, These men are the servants of the most high God, which shew unto us the way of salvation. And this did she many days. But Paul, being grieved, turned and said to the spirit, I command thee in the name of Jesus Christ to come out of her. And he came out the same hour. And when her masters saw that the hope of their gains was gone, they caught Paul and Silas, and drew them into the marketplace unto the rulers. —Acts 16:16-19

Paul went to Ephesus to preach. On his arrival he was helped by a young girl who told the people Paul was a man of God who had come to show them the way of salvation. Unknowingly she was a minister of Satan and for days she deceived him. Later Paul realized through supernatural means that a familiar spirit was working through her. He cast out the spirit. As a result, those who profited from her psychic ability had him thrown in jail. This girl was using familiar spirits for the following reasons.

She had supernatural knowledge. She was the first person to identify Paul as a man of God. She knew it supernaturally because she did not know them from anywhere.

She could predict the future. This ability had made her handlers rich in business because they had an upper hand.

Why was Paul initially deceived by her? I believe her supernatural knowledge and willingness to help her preach the Gospel deceived him. In so doing she won Paul's confidence.

11

Predicting the Future

Moreover, the LORD will also deliver Israel with thee into the hand of the Philistines: and to morrow shalt thou and thy sons be with me.

—1 Samuel 28:19

This finally brings us to the climax of the operation of familiar spirits. They want to predict your future and control your life.

The familiar spirit predicted the death of Saul and his sons. Supernatural knowledge won his confidence and prediction decided his future. The witch said, "You and your two sons will die tomorrow." He said nothing. Do you know why he said nothing? Because he thought it was a message from God. Words are seeds in the spirit realm, "A man's belly shall be satisfied with the fruit of his mouth; and with the increase of his lips shall he be filled. Death and life are in the power of the tongue: and they that love it shall eat the fruit thereof" (Proverbs 18:20-21).

Words are seeds that have the power to produce fruit. Jesus said, "The seed is the word of God" (Luke 8:11). Any word, irrespective of who spoke it, is a seed in the spirit realm. That is why "a man shall be satisfied with the fruit of his mouth." Our words are spiritual seeds, which eventually grow and produce fruit. That is why our words can shape our life experiences.

I once traveled to a certain country. At the immigration station they asked me what I did. I told them I was a minister. They mistook me for a government minister—not a minister of the Gospel. They gave me VIP treatment. I did not say anything because I am a minister and an ambassador for Christ.

Words can give life or death. "Death and life are in the power of the tongue." That is why you can kill or give life to your marriage by what you say.

Let's examine several ways through which familiar spirits speak to us and predict the future.

PREDICTION BY "MEN OF GOD"

A sister attended a prophetic meeting and a certain prophet said to her, "You will die in two months." She said, "I will *not* die. I *won't* die." The prophet said, "Are you challenging me? I said you *will* die; just wait and see if my words will not come to pass." You must be careful not to allow "men of God" to sow negative seeds in your life.

She was so scared that she came to see me for prayer. I told her she had allowed a familiar spirit to predict her future through a man of God. Jesus said, "The thief cometh not, but for to steal, and to kill, and to destroy: I am come that they might have life, and that they might have it more abundantly" (John 10:10).

I cancelled those evil words in Jesus' name. The date came and passed and she is still alive today. She almost allowed a familiar spirit to predict her future.

YOUR WIFE WILL DIE

A pastor I did not know approached me and told me he had a message from God for me. Because he was a pastor I decided to listen. He told me a couple of things that were true. After he said, "Pastor, I have a revelation."

I said, "What is the revelation?"

He said, "Your wife will die this year."

I immediately realized a familiar spirit was trying to predict my future. I said, "My wife will not die. She will live." I uprooted his evil prediction by countering it with a positive confession. God told Jeremiah, "I have put My words in your mouth ... to uproot" (see Jeremiah 1:9-10).

The pastor said to me, "Are you saying I am wrong?"

I answered, "You may be right but you didn't see well."

He asked me, "What do you mean I did not see well?"

I said, "The person you saw was not my wife. It was rather your wife." I knew he was a messenger of Satan.

He continued, "Are you saying what I saw is not true?"

I said, "It is true. It is only the identity of the person I dispute."

I cursed his evil words and refused to accept them. Do you know what happened? I am sad to say his wife did die that year. "Whoso diggeth a pit shall fall therein: and he that rolleth a stone, it will return upon him" (Proverbs 26:27). Make sure you uproot evil words with counter-confessions from the Scriptures.

PREDICTION BY STRANGERS

One day I was in traffic when a man approached my window and said, "I have a message from God for you." Immediately I knew a familiar spirit wanted to predict my future.

He was about to open his mouth when I said, "Shut up! Keep your words to yourself!" My heavenly Father has warned me to not talk to strangers and I take it seriously. "And a stranger will they not follow, but will flee from him: for they know not the voice of strangers" (John 10:5).

I have seen familiar spirits try to use strangers to divine, control, and predict the future of people. Familiar spirits will try to influence the course of your life: your marriage, health, finances, etc. They operate through negative words.

The devil tried to speak to Jesus through Peter and Jesus turned and said to him, "Get thee behind me, Satan." We must not allow strangers to minister to us.

PREDICTION BY WOLVES

> For I know this, that after my departing shall grievous wolves enter in among you, not sparing the flock.   —Acts 20: 29

Paul warned the church of Ephesus about the activity of wolves. These are people in congregations who mix with the flock to destroy or take advantage of them. Paul called them wolves. They are not there for the "grass" of the Word of God—they are there for blood, to take advantage of the sheep, congregation, or members of the church.

There are sometimes "spiritual people" in the church who claim the powers of the pastor. They usually do not join the leadership of the church but give private words of knowledge and begin to control other members of the church. They may instruct people to pray and fast because of prophecies and revelations they claim they have had. Sometimes they even exploit people sexually and financially.

They usually hide their operations from the pastor. Some of these people are controlled by familiar spirits. They gain control by divination and progress to control other members of the church through manipulation and prediction. From time to time I have encountered such people in our church.

PREDICTION THROUGH DREAMS

I once had a dream where a doctor presented me with a medical report. He said I was suffering from so-and-so disease. Immediately I woke up and cursed that evil dream. Jesus said, "The thief cometh not, but for to steal, and to kill, and to destroy: I am come that they might have life, and that they might have it more abundantly" (John 10:10).

Familiar spirits can manifest in your dreams and try to predict your future. For example, when you have a dream that you are being buried, it could be a prediction of your future in the spirit realm. It is said that a picture is worth a thousand words.

You must not allow evil words and images in dreams to take root. When you wake up you must curse them. You must say things like, "I curse this dream in the name of Jesus! I shall not die. I shall live and declare the works of the Lord. The Lord is my light and my salvation; whom shall I fear?"

You may have a dream that your two children are doing drugs. It could be a familiar spirit trying to seize control of their life by predicting their future. In a dream someone may tell you that you will never have a good marriage or you will find it difficult to conceive. Unfortunately many Christians say nothing after hearing or seeing a bad prediction of their future. When you wake up you should say something like, "My wife shall be as a fruitful vine by the sides of thine house: thy children like olive plants round about thy table" (Psalm 128:3).

Use the Word of God and confession to wage a good warfare. That's how you deal with familiar spirits.

12

FAMILIAR SPIRITS ARE RELIGIOUS

Because thou obeyedst not the voice of the LORD, nor executedst his fierce wrath upon Amalek, therefore hath the LORD done this thing unto thee this day.   —1 Samuel 28:18

A prophet came to see me concerning various problems he was having in his private life and ministry. Whilst praying for him I had a vision and saw him consulting the occult for power to divine and perform miracles.

I told him about this vision and he confessed to me that it was true. He was using familiar spirits to minister. I counseled him to repent and be a genuine

Christian. How could a minister of God with familiar spirits operate undetected?

Familiar spirits are difficult to detect because they are highly religious and like operating around churches and men of God. This serves as a camouflage for their operations. Because of this people who use familiar spirits can be confusing and controversial.

The familiar spirit that appeared to Saul was acting like a Christian counselor. He told him about the consequences of disobeying God. He reminded Saul of his disobedience to the Lord when he failed to destroy Agag, the Amalekite king, and all their goods.

Logically it is assumed that if someone advises you to obey God he must be from God. But it was a cover-up. They are wolves in sheep's clothing.

The Example of Paul

> And it came to pass, as we went to prayer, a certain damsel possessed with a spirit of divination met us, which brought her masters much gain by soothsaying: The same followed Paul and us, and cried, saying, These men are the servants of the most high God, which shew unto us the way of salvation. And this did she many days. But Paul, being grieved, turned and said to the spirit, I command thee in the name of Jesus Christ to come out of her. And he came out the same hour.   —Acts 16:16-18

When Paul arrived in Ephesus even the senior pastors didn't show up to help him. But a young girl with familiar spirits did. She went house to house evangelizing with Paul. She introduced him to the people and must have said things like, "George, meet Paul. He is a great man of God. He is here to preach and show us the way of salvation. Oh, Aunty Rose, meet Paul, a very great man of God."

What pastor would not be happy to have such a zealous member? I am sure she would have qualified to be one of the pastors in many churches. But it was all a scam. She was operating with familiar spirits under the guise of Christianity.

THE EXAMPLE OF BALAAM

> And the elders of Moab and the elders of Midian departed with the rewards of divination in their hand; and they came unto Balaam, and spake unto him the words of Balak. —Numbers 22:7

Balaam is a controversial prophet in the Scriptures. He was hired by Balak, the king of Israel, to curse Israel. He failed in cursing Israel because whenever he spoke, the curses were replaced by a blessing. Finally he advised Balaam to get the Moabite women to sleep with the children of Israel and God's curse would automatically come on them. Later Moses commanded these women to be slain, "Behold, these caused the children of Israel, through the counsel of Balaam, to commit trespass against the LORD in the matter of Peor, and there was a plague among the congregation of the LORD" (Numbers 31:16).

JOSHUA'S VERDICT ON BALAAM

Balaam also the son of Beor, the soothsayer, did the children of Israel slay with the sword among them that were slain by them.

—Joshua 13:22

According to Joshua, Balaam was a soothsayer because he had backslid.

PETER'S VERDICT ON BALAAM

But there were false prophets also among the people, even as there shall be false teachers among you, who privily shall bring in damnable heresies, even denying the Lord that bought them, and bring upon themselves swift destruction.   —2 Peter 2:1

Peter warned the church about the emergence of false prophets and teachers and cited Balaam as a specific example of a false prophet, "Which have forsaken the right way, and are gone astray, following the way of Balaam the son of Bosor, who loved the wages of unrighteousness" (2 Peter 2:15). It seems

Balaam started out as a genuine prophet because we are told he went astray. When he appears in Numbers 22 he had already backslidden. He had all the appearances of a genuine prophet, but he was using familiar spirits. Balaam was a mixture of several things.

Obedience and disobedience to God. Spiritual gifts and divination, service to God and service to God's enemies.

Spiritual counsel and demonic counsel; the love of God and the love for money. He could oscillate between genuine spiritual gifts and familiar spirits. He could also communicate with God and familiar spirits.

This is what makes some ministers of God look very confusing. They are a combination of God's power and familiar spirits.

Can two opposing spirits operate through a person? It's possible. Peter had a revelation through the Holy Spirit that Jesus was the Messiah, "And Jesus answered and said unto him, Blessed art thou, Simon Barjona: for flesh and blood hath not revealed it unto thee, but my Father which is in heaven" (Matthew 16:17).

Within a few minutes Jesus was rebuking Peter for allowing the devil to use him to advise Him against dying on the cross, "But he turned, and said unto Peter, Get thee behind me, Satan: thou art an offence unto me: for thou savourest not the things that be of God, but those that be of men" (Matthew 16:23).

Someone may say, "Oh! But Balaam could hear the voice of God." Even Nebuchadnezzar could hear the voice of God. Many Christians forget that God can speak to unbelievers. He was the one who had a vision of a statue, made of gold, brass, bronze, and clay mixed with iron. This vision about how world events will unfold was not given to a prophet. It was given to an unbeliever. God speaks to unbelievers.

When a person who used to operate in genuine spiritual gifts backslides, it is possible for the Holy Spirit to be replaced by an evil spirit. It happened to Saul when he backslid as the king of Israel. He ruled for forty years over Israel. But by the third year the Spirit of the Lord had left him. He had all the trappings of a king, but another spirit had replaced the Holy Spirit: "But the Spirit of the Lord departed from Saul, and an evil spirit from the Lord troubled him." Saul had backslid but he could still prophesy. The Holy Spirit had been replaced by another spirit, "And it came to pass on the morrow, that the evil spirit from God came upon Saul, and he prophesied in the midst of the house: and David played with his hand, as at other times: and there was a javelin in Saul's hand. And Saul cast the javelin; for he said, I will smite David even to the wall with it. And David avoided out of his presence twice" (1 Samuel 18:10-11). Love was also absent. Saul now wanted to murder David.

I am personally wary of people who exercise the gifts of the Spirit but lack the fruit of the Spirit. They don't impress me. You can have all the trappings of a pastor, but it's possible for the Holy Spirit to be replaced by another spirit. The person may be able to operate spiritual gifts but with another spirit.

13

THE SOURCE OF FAMILIAR SPIRITS

And the king said unto her, Be not afraid: for what sawest thou? And the woman said unto Saul, I saw gods ascending out of the earth.

—1 Samuel 28:13

There is something you must understand about demons. Where they originate from influences what they do. It is similar to where you buy a product can influence the quality of the product.

I once visited China and bought five brand-new phones from the street to give out as gifts. They looked like genuine, original phones. When I returned I tried making a call with one. After a few calls it wouldn't work again. I said, "Ah! What phone is this? Maybe it is a manufacturing mistake."

I took the second one and made two calls and it also went off. I tried the third, the fourth, and the fifth, and they all behaved the same way. I said to myself, *They seem to be disposable phones.* I will never buy a phone from the street in China again.

AIR FORCE DEMONS

One day a church member of mine who was dear to me fell critically ill. We decided to fast and pray for three days and seek the face of God for her healing. We rented a hotel room out of town and spent all the time interceding for her. On the third day we were standing and praying in a circle with our hands joined in intercession. Suddenly I fell into a trance and saw myself in the lower heavens. I saw our prayers being frustrated by evil spirits. God showed me the demons who were frustrating our prayers.

The evil spirits in the air are called principalities. They are the Air Force of the devil. Paul said, "We wrestle not against flesh and blood, but against principalities, against powers, against rulers of the darkness of this world, against spiritual wickedness in high places" (Ephesians 6:12).

High places means heavenly places. That is why principalities have the ability to intercept our prayers. They frustrated the prayers of Daniel. Daniel said, "In those days, I Daniel was mourning full three weeks, I ate no pleasant bread, neither came flesh nor wine into my mouth, neither did I anoint myself at all" (Daniel 10:2-3).

For twenty-one days there was no answer to his prayers. Later an angel appeared to him and told him the reason, "Then said he unto me, Fear not, Daniel: for from the first day that thou didst set thine heart to understand, and to chasten thyself before thy God, thy words were heard, and I am come for thy words. But the prince of the kingdom of Persia withstood me one and twenty days: but, lo, Michael, one of the chief princes, came to help me; and I remained there with the kings of Persia" (Daniel 10:12-13).

The prince of Persia frustrated Daniel's prayers. The word "prince" has the same meaning as the word "principality". One of the main functions of principalities is to intercept prayers in the heavens.

NAVY DEMONS

There are evil spirits that operate from the sea, water bodies, and rivers. Jesus encountered a storm on the sea when He was sailing to Gadara. His boat was nearly capsized, "As they sailed, He fell asleep: and there came down a storm of wind on the lake; and they were filled with water, and were in jeopardy. And they came to him, and awoke him, saying, Master, master, we perish. Then he arose, and rebuked the wind and the raging of the water; and they ceased, and there was a calm. And he said unto them, Where is your faith? And they being afraid wondered, saying one to another, What manner of man is this! For he commandeth even the winds and water, and they obey him" (Luke 8:23-25).

There were evil spirits in the sea and they did not like a preacher coming to preach. So they tried to create a storm to stop Him. Jesus rebuked the wind because this was not a natural wind; there were spirits behind it.

In the book of Job the devil sent a whirlwind to destroy his house, "And, behold, there came a great wind from the wilderness, and smote the four corners of the house, and it fell upon the young men, and they are dead; and I only am escaped alone to tell thee" (Job 1:19). This means the devil can use the elements.

THE CHURCH I PASTORED

I once took over a church that had an average attendance of about two hundred people. I asked God what I had to do to make the church grow. The following day I had a vision where I saw demons coming from the sea. They stood on the road and as the members were coming to church, they started driving them away. The Lord said to me, "The only place you have to direct your prayers to is the sea. The demons in the sea are fighting the church and preventing it from growing." From that day I started praying against these demons. All my "prayer bullets" were towards the sea. The church grew to thousands after a few years.

In the story of the mad man of Gadara, when Jesus finally landed on shores of Gadara the Bible says, "And all the devils besought him, saying, Send us into the swine, that we may enter into them" (Mark 5:12). Jesus gave them permission to enter the swine but that was not their final destination, "And forthwith Jesus gave them leave. And the unclean spirits went out, and entered into the swine: and the herd ran violently down a steep place into the sea, (they were about two thousand;) and were choked in the sea" (Mark 5:13).

The demons didn't want to remain in the pigs. Otherwise they would not have killed them. So why did they enter the pigs? I believe they used them as transportation to get to the sea. And do you know what happened? The people of the city told Jesus to leave the city. They did not want any church there. It seems to me the demons in the sea don't like church growth.

FAMILIAR SPIRITS COME FROM UNDERGROUND

And thou shalt be brought down, and shalt speak out of the ground, and thy speech shall be low out of the dust, and thy voice shall be, as of one that hath a familiar spirit, out of the ground, and thy speech shall whisper out of the dust.   —Isaiah 29:4

This prophecy is part of a prophecy God pronounced against a city called Ariel. God said Ariel would be brought down or destroyed and be like a familiar spirit. Note some of the features of familiar spirits in the verse. Familiar spirits come from underground, "thy voice shall be, as of one that hath a familiar spirit, out of the ground."

In the case of Saul the familiar spirits came from underground. "And the king said unto her, Be not afraid: for what sawest thou? And the woman said unto Saul, I saw gods ascending out of the earth" (1 Samuel 28:13).

I believe many sexual dreams are the activities of familiar spirits. Many people suffer from sexual attacks and even rape in dreams. I put familiar spirits at the top of such attacks.

14

IDENTIFYING FAMILIAR SPIRITS

Lest Satan should get an advantage of us: for we are not ignorant of his devices.

—2 Corinthians 2:11

For the word of God is quick, and powerful, and sharper than any twoedged sword, piercing even to the dividing asunder of soul and spirit, and of the joints and marrow, and is a discerner of the thoughts and intents of the heart. Neither is there any creature that is not manifest in his sight: but all things are naked and opened unto the eyes of him with whom we have to do.

—Hebrews 4:12-13

To deal with familiar spirits you must first be able to identify them. Identification is the act of finding who someone or what something is. Identification is crucial in today's world because of terrorism. The ability to identify terrorists before they strike is critical.

AT THE AIRPORT

Once I was late for a flight. As I looked at the long queue going through security I knew I could miss my flight. I prayed and asked the Lord to help me. After the prayer a man walked up to me and told me I had been randomly selected for special security screening. My body and luggage were scanned for any suspicious items or material. The good thing was I skipped the long queue and was able to catch the flight. God answered my prayer but in a very unusual way.

THE WORD IS A SCANNER

The Word of God can act like a scanner. It has the ability to scan spirit, soul, and body. It can scan the spirit realm and identify familiar spirits. In the book of Hebrews we learn about the scanning abilities of God's Word.

First of all it pierces, or has the ability to "scan" the three dimensions of man: spirit, soul, and body (joints and marrow). Secondly, everything is "naked" before the Word. It has the ability to go below the surface and reveal the true nature of everything. Thirdly, everything is opened before the Word, meaning nothing can be concealed or hidden from the Word.

FAMILIAR SPIRITS CAN BE IDENTIFIED BY THE WORD

> And when they shall say unto you, Seek unto them that have familiar spirits, and unto wizards that peep, and that mutter: should not a people seek unto their God? for the living to the dead? To the law and to the testimony: if they speak not according to this word, it is because there is no light in them.   —Isaiah 8:19-20

Let us look closely at this Scripture. First of all it asks a rhetorical question by warning us not to be enticed to practice necromancy: "should not a people seek unto their God? for the living to the dead?" We should be seeking answers from God—not the dead. This is because the Word of God forbids necromancy or communicating with the dead, "There shall not be found among you any one that maketh his son or his daughter to pass through the fire, or that useth divination, or an observer of times, or an enchanter, or a witch, or a charmer, or a consulter with familiar spirits, or a wizard, or a necromancer" (Deuteronomy 18:10-11).

The second thing we learn is that spiritual experiences, no matter how powerful, must always be judged in the light of the Scriptures. We cannot place a higher value on our experience than the Word, "To the law and to the testimony: if they speak not according to this word, it is because there is no light in them."

The "law and the testimony" refers to the Word of God. Anything that is not consistent with the Scriptures lacks divine light and must be dismissed.

THE HIDDEN GOLD

A woman once told me she had been communicating with her dead mother through a certain pastor. Her deceased mum had shown her where she had hidden some gold. They had gone to dig the place and could not locate it, so they needed further directions. I told her she had been consulting familiar spirits. This was inconsistent with the Scriptures and even simple logic. How come the mother did not show them the location of the gold when she was alive? It did not even make sense.

15

THE ANOINTING

"These things have I written unto you concerning them that seduce you. But the anointing which ye have received of him abideth in you, and ye need not that any man teach you: but as the same anointing teacheth you of all things, and is truth, and is no lie, and even as it hath taught you, ye shall abide in him." —1 John 2:26-27

A BUSINESS OPPORTUNITY

A man came to present a glorious business opportunity to a woman I knew. She was very impressed but I told her, "This man is a con man and wants to swindle you." She asked why and I told her I knew it by the anointing.

"How do you know?" she probed.

I said, "Something deep in me tells me something is wrong."

I couldn't prove it but it was a deep gut feeling. That thing that people call "something" is called the anointing.

The anointing means the power of God and it can manifest in different ways. There is an anointing to preach, teach, and heal. There is also a specific anointing to detect deception. Let's examine these verses.

First of all John warned the church about the rise in deception, "These things have I written unto you concerning them that seduce you." Secondly, he reminded them that there is a particular anointing in every Christian, "But the anointing which ye have received of him abideth in you." Thirdly, this anointing is specifically designed to detect deception and acts as a scanner in your spirit. It teaches us to distinguish between the truth of God's Word and lies in any given situation, "the same anointing teacheth you of all things, and is truth, and is no lie."

For example, when a man looks at you and says, "Baby, any time I see you I forget my own mother's name." Forget about the sweet words; rely on the anointing to discern whether he is a good person. It will help you to distinguish a good man from a bad man, a good opportunity from a bad opportunity, and a familiar spirit from the Spirit of God.

Some people interpret this Scripture to mean no one should teach us the Word or we don't need to go to church. It's not taking about church; it's talking about deception. Fortunately this anointing has been given to every single member of the church. Remember, John was addressing the *whole* church.

I once watched a film where terrorists hijacked a plane. Some people needed medical attention so a medical team was sent onboard. The star posed as one of the members of the medical team. As he was about to enter the plane the leader who was standing at the door said, "Mister, I don't like your face." He asked, "Why?" The man replied, "I don't know, but I just don't like your face." Something told him all was not right. He did not allow the star to board the plane. He had to use another means.

Someone may say, "But I know people who have wrong convictions." I also know people like that. Wrong convictions are developed when we ignore the gentle promptings of the Holy Spirit when He pulls on our heart. Over time we lose this anointing or conviction.

This anointing can be corrupted and be called a "sixth sense." If a terrorist can have this "questionable anointing," then we as the children of God have no excuse.

16

A Second Opinion

This is the third time I am coming to you. In the mouth of two or three witnesses shall every word be established.   —2 Corinthians 13:1

For you to establish the truth about a situation you may have to confirm it with two or three witnesses or seek a second opinion. These should be spiritually mature and experienced people.

Let the prophets speak two or three, and let the other judge. —1 Corinthians 14:29

This verse tells us we can rely on other spiritually mature people to judge spiritual experiences. This is even more crucial when it concerns someone you know. Especially when that person's fruit or character is not consistent with a vision or dream you have had about him.

For example, if I had a dream that my enemy was one of my fellow pastors whom I have known for many years and can vouch for his integrity, I would not accept it. I cannot assess him based on a single dream. This is because a familiar spirit can impersonate him, "Against an elder receive not an accusation, but before two or three witnesses" (1 Timothy 5:19). That is why you must be careful not to use one dream or experience to form an opinion of people whose track record and history is inconsistent with a revelation you have had about them.

A man told me he was going to divorce his new wife because of a dream he had. In the dream his wife was defecating on him. I advised him not to be hasty to form an opinion about someone he had known for some time based on one single dream. It had to be corroborated by other things. This verse tells us we can rely on other spiritually mature people to judge spiritual experiences.

How to Deal with Familiar Spirits: The Fruit of the Spirit

The fruit of the Spirit helps us to know whether the Holy Spirit is present in a given situation. The evidence of a fruit is stronger than the evidence of the leaves.

If I were to see a strange tree with apples, I would conclude it was an apple tree although it may be very different. In the same way the fruit of the Spirit helps us to know whether the Holy Spirit is present, "Beware of false prophets, which come to you in sheep's clothing, but inwardly they are ravening wolves. Ye shall know them by their fruits. Do men gather grapes of thorns, or figs of thistles?" (Matthew 7:15-16).

Jesus said the fruit of the Spirit helps you to know what you are dealing with, "But the fruit of the Spirit is love, joy, peace, longsuffering, gentleness, goodness, faith, meekness, temperance: against such there is no law" (Galatians 5:22-23). We can tell the presence of familiar spirits by the fruit they leave behind. They leave the opposite of the fruit of the Spirit.

Hatred replaces love; sadness, joy; strife, peace; impatience, longsuffering; cruelty, gentleness; evil, goodness; unbelief, faith; pride, meekness; and a lack of self-control replaces temperance.

Saul's family was plagued with negative fruit after consulting the familiar spirit. The experience was phenomenal but the results were disastrous. We must measure people by the fruit they leave behind.

After Saul's death there was strife and hatred between his house and David's house. Sadness came to the family because of the death of a father and his two sons. Evil, pride, etc., came to his family. The overall contribution of the familiar spirit was negative.

17

PRAYER

Wherefore God also hath highly exalted him, and given him a name which is above every name: That at the name of Jesus every knee should bow, of things in heaven, and things in earth, and things under the earth; and that every tongue should confess that Jesus Christ is Lord, to the glory of God the Father.

—Philippians 2:9-11

Familiar spirits come from underground. That is one reason why the name of Jesus works under the earth, "That at the name of Jesus every knee should bow, of things in heaven, and things in earth, and things under the earth."

For if God spared not the angels that sinned,
but cast them down to hell, and delivered them
into chains of darkness, to be reserved unto
judgment.   —2 Peter 2:4

I want you to notice that the angels that sinned were
imprisoned underground: in hell, "Hell from beneath
is moved for thee to meet thee at thy coming" (Isaiah
14:9). The knowledge about the source of familiar
spirits is key because it makes our prayer precise and
effective.

SNIPER

Snipers use very few bullets because their focus
and aim are precise. When our prayer is targeted at
the source of familiar spirits we can act like spiritual snipers. Our prayers can be specific and precise
because knowledge gives us such clarity and focus. We
will not be shadow boxing, "I therefore so run, not as
uncertainly; so fight I, not as one that beateth the air"
(1 Corinthians 9:26).

THE WOMAN WHO HAD SEX WITH DOGS

While ministering I had a specific word of knowledge about someone who had sex in their dreams with
a dog. A woman told me she was the one. Can you
imagine a dog and a human? When I laid hands on her

and prayed she started manifesting like a dog. I cast out the evil spirit and she was delivered.

Some people who have been victims of familiar spirits have prayed and had no respite. They still see themselves communicating with the dead or sleeping with people in dreams, etc. I believe if their prayers were a little bit more precise they would receive answers. There are several things we can do with prayer to prevail. I want to discuss some.

1. CLOSE EVERY DEMONIC PIT IN THE NAME OF JESUS

> And the fifth angel sounded, and I saw a star fall from heaven unto the earth: and to him was given the key of the bottomless pit. And he opened the bottomless pit; and there arose a smoke out of the pit, as the smoke of a great furnace; and the sun and the air were darkened by reason of the smoke of the pit. And there came out of the smoke locusts upon the earth: and unto them was given power, as the scorpions of the earth have power.
>
> —Revelation 9:1-3

This is because demonic pits exist and they can be closed or opened with the name of Jesus, "And he opened the bottomless pit." This Scripture reminds us of the existence of demonic puts. These pits can be closed or opened. This particular pit was closed until an angel opened it with a key: "and to him was given the key of the bottomless pit"; "and he opened the bottomless pit." Spirits like great locusts came out when this was done. The name of Jesus is so powerful. It has authority in heaven, on earth, and under the earth. It also has the power to bind and loose or open and close.

Jesus said to Peter, "And I will give unto thee the keys of the kingdom of heaven: and whatsoever thou shalt bind on earth shall be bound in heaven: and whatsoever thou shalt loose on earth shall be loosed in heaven" (Matthew 16:19). This key is the name of Jesus. If I were to use the name of Jesus, I would say something like, "I close every demonic pit in the name of Jesus and bind every familiar spirit in Jesus' name."

2. USE THE BLOOD OF JESUS

The blood was used during the Passover to prevent the death angel from entering the house of the Jews. Because of this I could pray and say, "I seal every satanic pit with the blood and cover this ground with the blood." This will prevent familiar spirits from coming out.

3. THE BLOOD CAN LOCK SPIRITUAL DOORS

And all the firstborn in the land of Egypt shall die, from the firstborn of Pharaoh that sitteth upon his throne, even unto the firstborn of the maidservant that is behind the mill; and all the firstborn of beasts. And there shall be a great cry throughout all the land of Egypt, such as there was none like it, nor shall be like it any more. But against any of the children of Israel shall not a dog move his tongue, against man or beast: that ye may know how that the LORD doth put a difference between the Egyptians and Israel.   —Exodus 11:5-7

Just as we lock physical doors before we sleep, through prayer we can also lock spiritual doors before we sleep. During the Passover the blood was put on the lintels of the houses of the Jews to prevent the angel of death, a spirit, from entering the houses of the Israelites. The Israelites were spared but the firstborn of every animal or human of the Egyptians died. The blood spiritually locked the doors.

WOMAN WITHOUT MENSES

This reminds me of the case of a married woman in her late thirties who had never menstruated before and as a result had no children. Every time it was time for her menses, a huge man in red shorts would appear in her dreams and have sex with her.

I prayed with her and locked every demonic pit with the blood. A few days later she had her first menses and a couple of months later she became pregnant. The familiar spirits were locked out. It's time to lock them out.

When we pray we usually say, "Lord, we cover the roof with the blood; we cover the walls with the blood; we cover the doors with the blood." We fail to cover the ground because many do not know that familiar spirits come from underground. Because of this they can operate freely. That is why the name of Jesus binds things under the earth.

HOW TO APPLY THE BLOOD

Your tongue is the brush that applies the blood of Jesus. That is why confessing and declaring the word is key, "If we confess our sins, he is faithful and just to forgive us our sins, and to cleanse us from all unrighteousness" (1 John 1:9).

Confession applies the blood for us to be cleansed. Confession will also release the blood to lock satanic pits.

BLOOD ON MY HANDS

When I am about to lay hands on and pray for the sick, I usually ask the Lord to sanctify my hands, eyes, and ears with the blood. This is to prevent spiritual contamination, "Lay hands suddenly on no man, neither be partaker of other men's sins: keep thyself pure" (1 Timothy 5:22).

One day something happened that strengthened my faith in the blood and confession. Someone took several pictures of me at a meeting and in all the shots my right hand seemed to be dripping with blood. Confession and prayer release the blood.

18

UPROOTING AND PLANTING

Now the parable is this: The seed is the word of God.   —Luke 8:11

A man's belly shall be satisfied with the fruit of his mouth; and with the increase of his lips shall he be filled. Death and life are in the power of the tongue: and they that love it shall eat the fruit thereof.   —Proverbs 18:20-21

Words are seeds in the realm of the spirit. Jesus said, "The seed is the word of God" (Luke 8:11). A seed is anything that has the ability to multiply itself. Words eventually become fruit, "they that love it shall eat the fruit thereof." For example, when I became born again I confessed Jesus as my Lord and

Savior. Some of my friends doubted my sincerity, but after some time they saw the fruit of the Spirit manifest in my life. My confession changed my life.

WORDS CAN MINISTER LIFE OR DEATH

Words also have the ability to produce life or death, "Death and life are in the power of the tongue." We can feed or starve things to death with our words. You can kill or give life to your marriage by the words you speak.

When we talk about our pain, we feed our pain and it grows bigger. But when we decide to forgive and forget, we starve our pain and it begins to diminish. A familiar spirit can plant seeds in your life through the following means.

1. FAMILIAR SPIRITS CAN USE PEOPLE TO SPEAK TO US

In the case of Saul, the familiar spirit used the witch to pronounce death on him.

2. FAMILIAR SPIRITS CAN SPEAK TO US THROUGH DREAMS AND VISIONS

I once dreamt that someone approached me and said I was going to die. When I woke up I rebuked the evil words in Jesus' name. "Another parable put he forth unto them, saying, The kingdom of heaven is likened unto a man which sowed good seed in his field: But while men slept, his enemy came and sowed tares among the wheat, and went his way" (Matthew 13:24-25).

In the parable of the tares the enemy, the devil, sowed evil seeds or tares. I want you to notice when this activity was carried out, "While men slept, his enemy came and sowed tares among the wheat." One way the devil ministers to us is in dreams—when we are asleep. The principle here is that words can be sown as seeds in dreams.

3. BACK TO THE PAST

Sometimes we may already have allowed familiar spirits to speak to us through dreams and people. This is because we may not have even known the spiritual implication. The good thing is, in the spirit realm every satanic word or seed can be uprooted although it may have occurred in the past. Spiritually we can uproot demonic seeds through the power of words. Prayer and confession can do this, "Death and life are in the power of the tongue."

Then the LORD put forth his hand, and touched my mouth. And the LORD said unto me, Behold, I have put my words in thy mouth. See, I have this day set thee over the nations and over the kingdoms, to root out, and to pull

down, and to destroy, and to throw down, to
build, and to plant.   —Jeremiah 1:9-10

God touched the mouth of Jeremiah and told
him about the power of words. From this Scripture
the power words can be grouped into two categories:
destructive and constructive words.

Destructive Words

The destructive capabilities of words include:
rooting out, throwing down, and destroying. The
constructive capabilities are building and planting.

You can destroy the works of familiar spirits. You
can root out bad dreams and evil words that familiar
spirits have spoken against you. Jesus said, "Every
plant, which my heavenly Father hath not planted,
shall be rooted up" (Matthew 15:13).

Let me give you an example. Suppose someone
told me I would never have a good marriage. I can
destroy those words by saying, "I refuse these evil words
concerning my marriage, in Jesus' name. I uproot them
with the name and blood of Jesus and curse them to
wither and die to the root." Through faith the effect of
those words can be destroyed, although they may have
been spoken twenty years ago.

THE EXAMPLE OF JESUS

> Then Peter took him, and began to rebuke him, saying, Be it far from thee, Lord: this shall not be unto thee. But he turned, and said unto Peter, Get thee behind me, Satan: thou art an offence unto me: for thou savourest not the things that be of God, but those that be of men.
> —Matthew 16:22-23

When Peter tried to dissuade Jesus from going to the cross, Jesus rebuked the spirit that was influencing him. He said, "Get thee behind me, Satan." He did not keep silent or say in His head, *I don't agree with this.* When Peter spoke Jesus immediately uprooted the negative words with counter words. That is why we must root out demonic seeds and trees from our lives.

CONSTRUCTIVE WORDS

We must also deliberately cultivate good seeds in our lives because no beautiful garden develops by itself. It is a deliberate effort, which involves the removal of weeds and the planting of beautiful flowers. After a negative word has been destroyed a good seed must be planted in its place. This is because nature abhors a vacuum.

Using the marriage example I just spoke about, I would not end at destroying the negative words. I would proceed to sow positive words, such as, "My marriage will be blessed, and I will experience peace and love, in Jesus' name." You will be planting good seeds in the spirit realm.

CONCLUSION

We know that whosoever is born of God
sinneth not; but he that is begotten of God
keepeth himself, and that wicked one toucheth
him not.   —1 John 5:18

Holiness has always been and will always be the
first line of defense against the devil.

It is my prayer that this book has shed light on
familiar spirits, a category of demons whose activities
have been shrouded in mystery. Through knowledge,
prayer, and faith, I believe every familiar spirit will
bow down to you, in Jesus' name.

God bless you.

ABOUT THE AUTHOR

KAKRA BAIDEN

Many years ago the Lord Jesus Christ appeared in a vision to Kakra Baiden and called him into the ministry as a prophet, teacher, and miracle worker. He is also known as "the walking Bible" for his supernatural ability to preach and teach the Bible from memory.

Pastor Baiden is an architect by profession and serves as a bishop of the Lighthouse Chapel International denomination. He has trained many pastors and planted many churches within the Lighthouse denomination.

Currently he is the senior pastor of the Morning Star Cathedral, Lighthouse Chapel International, Accra. He is a sought-after revivalist and conference speaker.

He is also the president of Airpower, a ministry through which he touches the world through radio and TV broadcasts, books, CDs, videos, the Internet, and international conferences dubbed "The Airpower Conference." He has ministered the Word on every continent and is also the author of the best-selling book, *Squatters*.

Pastor Baiden is married to Lady Rev. Dr. Ewuradwoa Baiden and they have four children.

For additional information on Kakra Baiden's books
and messages (CDs and DVDs),
write to any of these addresses:

US
26219 Halbrook Glen Lane
Katy, TX 77494

UK
32 Tern Road
Hampton, Hargate
Cambridgeshire
Pe78DG

GHANA
P.O. Box SK 1067
Sakumono Estates, Tema
Ghana-West Africa

E-MAIL: info@kakrabaiden.org
WEBSITE: www.kakrabaiden.org
FACEBOOK: www.facebook.com/KakraBaiden
TWITTER: www.twitter.com/ProphetKakraB

www.ingramcontent.com/pod-product-compliance
Lightning Source LLC
Chambersburg PA
CBHW071613040426
42452CB00008B/1334